S·P·O·R·T·S
Heroes AND Heroines

By
Eugene Coco

kidsbooks
Incorporated

Cover and interior photos:
AP/Wide World Photos

Copyright © 1993 Kidsbooks, Inc.
3535 West Peterson Avenue
Chicago, IL 60659

ISBN: 1-56156-206-8

Manufactured in the United States of America

TABLE OF CONTENTS

INTRODUCTION

It wasn't long ago that Larry Bird and Magic Johnson were considered the best basketball players in the NBA. No one could pass a basketball like Magic, and no one could nail a 3-pointer like Bird. Together, they dominated the 1980's, winning eight NBA championships between them. Then along came Michael Jordan. With his high flying dunks and in-your-face defense, Michael has won three consecutive NBA championships. But now, in only his first year in the NBA, Shaquille O'Neal is doing things with a basketball that no other player over seven feet tall has ever done. Whether it be hitting the open man on a fast break, scoring in the low post, or swatting away jump shots, "Shaq" is already one of the most dominating basketball players ever to play the game, and he is sure to make the Orlando Magic one of the most exciting teams to watch in the 1990's.

The hardest battle that track star Gail Devers had to face in preparing for the 1992 Olympics was not on the field, but in the hospital. In 1990, diagnosed with a life-threatening thyroid condition called Graves' disease, Gail nearly gave up all hope of ever running again. But with the help of Coach Bobby Kersee and physical therapist Bob Forster, Gail not only made the team, but won a gold medal in the 100-meter dash in the 1992 Olympics. She is also the current American record holder in the 100-meter hurdles.

One of the youngest quarterbacks in the history of the National Football League to guide his team to a Super Bowl victory, Troy Aikman, just 26 years old, is quickly living up to his potential as the number one pick in the 1989 draft. With a strong arm, quick release, and uncanny ability to find his receivers down field, Troy Aikman is setting his sights on another Super Bowl ring in the upcoming season. Mature beyond his years, Troy's greatest asset may be his "coolness" in the pocket. He never seems to get rattled and can always be counted on to make the right decision under pressure.

Ever since Chris Evert began slipping from the ranks of women's professional tennis in the late 1980's, Americans have been searching for someone to take her place. In 1989, that "someone" came along. It was a 13-year-old "wonder kid" from Florida named Jennifer Capriati. In 1990, Jennifer burst onto the tennis scene at Wimbledon, lasting until the fourth round. She possesses a powerful forehand, precise ground strokes, and one of the best serves on the women's tour in years. And while Jennifer has yet to reach number one in the rankings, this past summer she did walk away with an Olympic gold medal.

For years, Wayne Gretzky was the most valuable player in the National Hockey League. He won more scoring titles than anyone in league history, surpassed Gordie Howe for career points, and led the Edmonton Oilers to four Stanley Cup victories. Now it's Mario Lemieux's turn. Wearing his famous number 66, in tribute to Gretzky's number 99, Mario was a star the minute he stepped onto the ice in 1984.

Last year's Conn Smythe Trophy winner, Mario's size—he's 6'4" and weighs 225 pounds—speed, and pinpoint passing make him almost impossible to defend against, and the Pittsburgh Penguins are two-time Stanley Cup Champions because of him.

Although the USA's Women's Basketball Team came away from the 1992 Olympic Games with only a bronze medal, Teresa Edwards established herself as the best female basketball player in the world today. A gold medalist in the 1984 and 1988 Olympics, Teresa admits that not winning a third gold medal in 1992 was a disappointment to her, but she has her sights set on making the 1996 team. Teresa currently plays professional basketball in Europe and Japan, where she is one of the most popular American stars.

Ken Griffey, Jr., in only his fourth major league season, is the one baseball player most often compared to Hall of Famers Willie Mays and Mickey Mantle for his all-around ability. A rare combination of size, speed, and power, Ken Griffey, Jr., is regarded by many baseball experts as the most complete player in the game today. This triple Golden Glove award winner can score with his defense as well as his bat. A three-time All-Star, Ken is the main reason why the Seattle Mariners are one of the most feared young teams in the league today.

Over the past decade, women have made tremendous strides in sports, and most experts readily agree that it's just a matter of time before they equal or surpass the accomplishments set by their male counterparts in such sports as track and field, golf, and swimming. But if you were to name the one sport where women would seemingly have the most difficulty competing with men, it would have to be hockey. That has all changed. When the Tampa Bay Lightning announced last year that they had signed Manon Rheaume to a contract, it was thought to be purely a promotional tactic. But Manon proved them wrong. With her lightning-fast reflexes and ability to cover the net with uncanny speed, Manon has shown that she's right where she belongs—in the NHL.

As we move further on into the 1990's, these young stars will be leading the way. Their desire to win, their commitment to excellence, and their ability to make their teammates better players are just some of the qualities which separate them from the rest of the athletes in their sports. As these stars soar to newer and greater heights, the 1990's will undoubtedly prove to be a record-breaking decade.

CHAPTER ONE

Shaquille O'Neal

❖ ❖ ❖ ❖ ❖ ❖ ❖ ❖

The NBA's Rising Star

Shaquille Rashaun O'Neal was born in Newark, New Jersey, in 1972. In Arabic, Shaquille's first name means "little one" and his second name means "warrior". Shaquille certainly plays basketball like a warrior, but as for being a "little one," nothing could be further from the truth.

When Shaquille was 12, he moved with his family to an Army base in Wildflecken, West Germany. Though Shaquille missed his friends, moving was the best thing that could have happened to him.

By the time Shaquille was 13 years old, he stood 6'6", weighed 235 pounds, and wore a size 17 shoe.

"We'd buy him pants on the Army post on Saturday," said his father, "and the next Friday, they wouldn't fit."

Shaquille was almost 14 when he met Dale Brown, the head basketball coach at Louisiana State University. Coach Brown was in Germany giving a basketball clinic when Shaquille asked him how he could improve his game. When

Shaq swings from the rim after one of his famous slam dunks!

Coach Brown found out how old Shaquille was, he began recruiting Shaquille to play at L.S.U., even though he wasn't even in high school yet!

In 1987, Shaquille and his family moved back to the United States. They lived in San Antonio, Texas, where Shaquille went to Cole High School. By the time Shaquille was a junior, he was 6'10" and weighed 250 pounds. He led Cole High to a 32-1 record and then on to the State Championships. In his senior year, Cole High went undefeated, with a 36-0 record, and won the Texas state title. Because of his size, speed, and quickness, Shaquille was the most sought-after high school player in the country. Shaquille could have gone to any college he wanted, but he had his mind and heart set on playing for his friend Coach Brown at L.S.U.

When Shaquille joined the Tigers of L.S.U. in the fall of 1989, they were one of the teams most experts picked to win the National Championship. They had All-American guard Chris Jackson to go along with Shaquille, as well as 7' power-forward Stanley Roberts.

In high school, Shaquille was the focal point of the offense, but it was a different story in college. Everything worked around guard Chris Jackson, and Shaquille was asked to play more defense, set picks, and rebound. It took him a while to adjust to being "just another player" on a team. And although Shaquille averaged 14 points and 12 rebounds per game, and blocked 115 shots (a Southeastern Conference record), his freshman year proved to be a disappointing one, as the Tigers were eliminated from the NCAA Tournament in the first round.

During the summer of 1990, Shaquille played in the National Sports Festival and was easily the most valuable

**Rookie of the Year Shaquille O'Neal is an
awesome defender.**

player there. He averaged 24.5 points and 13.8 rebounds per game, often toying with the other college players who opposed him. Most coaches agreed that, if he wanted to, Shaquille could play in the NBA, but he was looking forward to his sophomore year at L.S.U.

When Shaquille returned to college in the fall, Chris Jackson had left school to play in the NBA, and Stanley Roberts had been ruled academically ineligible to play. Coach Brown named "Shaq" captain, and told him the Tigers "were in his hands." Shaquille responded by averaging 27.6 points and 14.7 rebounds per game, and was voted Player of the Year. Despite offers that might have enticed him to leave school early, Shaq stayed one more year at L.S.U. But with the lack of competition, and nothing else to prove, Shaquille decided to turn pro at the end of his junior year.

The Orlando Magic made Shaquille the highest-paid rookie in league history when they picked him first in the 1992 draft. In an exhibition game against the Olympic Dream Team, made up of some of the best basketball players in the NBA, Shaquille scored 39 points and pulled down 26 rebounds. Superstar Magic Johnson couldn't believe that someone as big as Shaquille could handle a basketball so well.

At 7'1" and nearly 300 pounds, Shaquille towered over most of the opposing centers he faced. But size isn't everything, as he soon found out. Playing against veterans such as Patrick Ewing, David Robinson, and Robert Parrish, Shaquille would often force his shots, get into foul trouble, and end up on the bench. But with each game, Shaquille learned something new, and by mid-season, he was averaging nearly 24 points and 14 rebounds per game, numbers good enough to get him voted to the starting center position for the East in the NBA All-Star game.

Orlando was one of the worst teams in the NBA last year. But with Shaquille leading the way, they improved their record to just under .500, and missed the play-offs in a tie-breaker with the Indiana Pacers.

Shaquille finished the season averaging 23.4 points and 13.9 rebounds per game, and was the runaway Rookie of the Year.

CHAPTER TWO

Gail Devers

Track and Field's Comeback Queen

Gail Devers first started running track as a junior at Sweetwater High School in National City, California. At age 16, Gail's fastest time in the 100-meter dash was 11.69 seconds. In her senior year, Gail decided that she wanted to try the 100-meter hurdles as well, in order to help build up her strength and endurance. Not only did Gail run a remarkable best time of 14.32 seconds in the hurdles, but the extra training enabled her to bring down her time in the 100-meter dash to 11.51 seconds. Gail's speed, strength, and versatility brought her track offers from major colleges around the country. After months of agonizing over where to enroll, Gail decided to stay close to home, and attend U.C.L.A.

Gail was at U.C.L.A. from 1985–88, and each year she improved her time in both the dash and the hurdles. As a senior, Gail won the NCAA title, and also took the 100 meter hurdles in a then U.S. record 12.61 seconds. With the

Gail Deevers flies over any hurdle that gets in her way.

1988 Olympic trials only a short time away, Gail seemed a sure bet to make the team and win a medal. That's when her troubles began.

Just before the Olympic trials, Gail started having breathing problems and difficulty sleeping. She also had frequent memory lapses, and her weight fluctuated uncontrollably. But Gail waited to see a doctor until after the trials were over. She had qualified for the 100-meter hurdles, but not the 100-meter dash.

Gail was diagnosed as having bronchial asthma, a disease that caused her to hyperventilate on the track. However, she kept her plans to attend the 1988 Olympics in Seoul. Once there, Gail suffered migraine headaches and had trouble eating. She did not make the Olympic finals, and returned home to take a couple of months off to rest. But even this didn't make her feel better. Frustrated at not being able to compete at the high level that she was used to, Gail was going to quit running track for good. But Coach Bobby Keresy convinced her to see a thyroid specialist first.

In September of 1990, Gail Devers was finally correctly diagnosed as having Graves' disease.

"The doctor who diagnosed the Graves' disease said I was two and a half weeks away from it being cancerous," she said. "If it would have been cancerous, it would have been irreversible."

Gail began radiation treatment almost immediately, though doctors told her that the chances of her returning for the 1991 track season were remote. Still, Gail remained hopeful. Though the radiation treatment stopped her excessive thyroid activity, it did produce severe blisters and boils on her feet. Things got so bad that Gail couldn't walk more than a few feet without screaming in pain.

Gail Deevers takes the gold in the 100 meter!

"I was approaching the point where they would have had to amputate my feet if I had not gone back to the doctor," she said.

That was in early March. Gail's new medication healed her feet, and in April, she walked around the track at U.C.L.A. in her socks. She called it her first "workout" in over a year. While it was difficult for Gail to get focused on running again, her desire and will to prove that she belonged with the elite of the track world was enough to motivate her.

In June of 1991, Gail ran a 13.28 time in the 100-meter hurdles at the Modesto Invitational, her first sanctioned meet in over a year. Coach Kersee called it a "miracle" when Gail came in second at the World Championships in Tokyo in the 100-meter hurdles with a remarkable time of 12.83. Then in September, Gail set the U.S. record at 12.48, breaking the previous record she shared with Jackie Joyner-Kersee.

The 1992 Olympics were only a year away, and though Gail was content with setting her sights on the 100-meter hurdles, Coach Kersee thought that she should run the 100-meter dash as well. Gail easily made the finals in Barcelona in both events.

As Gail stood at the starting line in the 100-meter dash, her thoughts were on the upcoming 100-meter hurdles the next day. To finish in the top five would be enough for her, as favorites Katrin Krabbe of Germany and Gwen Torrence of the U.S., stood beside her. To everyone's amazement, Gail won the dash in 10.82 seconds, edging out Irina Privalova of Russia and Juliet Cuthbert of Jamaica!

But when it came to the 100-meter hurdles, Gail clipped her foot on the last hurdle in the finals, and came in fifth. Though she was disappointed in not winning a second gold medal, Gail will always be remembered as having accomplished the greatest comeback in track and field history!

CHAPTER THREE

Troy Aikman

✧ ✧ ✧ ✧ ✧ ✧ ✧ ✧ ✧

The Dallas Cowboys' "Coolest" Quarterback

Troy Aikman grew up in the small town of Cerritos, California, and by the time he turned 16, was one of the best all-around athletes at Henryetta High School. Though he was a stand-out star in both baseball and basketball, Troy's first love was football.

In his senior year at Henryetta High, Troy earned All-State honors, and was one of the most highly recruited high school quarterbacks to ever come out of California. When it was time for him to select which college he was going to attend, Troy surprised everyone by deciding to play for Coach Barry Switzer at the University of Oklahoma.

Troy was an exceptional athlete, at 6'4" and 200 pounds. He was faster than most wide receivers, could throw a football nearly 80 yards, and possessed leadership qualities well beyond his years. But Oklahoma's game plan stressed

Superstar quarterback Troy Aikman led the Cowboys to victory in the Super Bowl.

the run, not the pass. They employed a wishbone offense, where Troy would either run with the football, or hand off to one of his three running backs. It was clear from the start that Troy's talents were wasted in Coach Switzer's system.

Ironically, Troy was injured in his sophomore year and missed almost the entire season. During that time, he decided to leave the University of Oklahoma and transfer to U.C.L.A., where Coach Terry Donoughe employed a more wide open, pass-oriented offense.

In 1988, his first year at U.C.L.A., Troy led the Bruins to a victory in the Aloha Bowl. Troy topped that in 1989 by "passing" the Bruins to a Cotton Bowl win. In his two years at U.C.L.A., Troy completed 64.8 percent of his passes for 5,298 yards and 41 touchdowns, while throwing only 17 interceptions. Troy finished his collegiate career as the third highest-rated passer in NCAA history, while guiding the Bruins to a 20–4 record. As a senior, Troy was a consensus All-American, and was the first player selected by the Dallas Cowboys in the 1989 NFL draft.

The Dallas Cowboys, once known as "America's Team," had fallen on hard times in the 1980's. In 1989, Jerry Jones, an Arkansas businessman, bought the Cowboys, and promised the city of Dallas that he would bring them a championship. The first thing that Jones did was hire University of Miami Head Coach Jimmy Johnson, who had a 52–9 career record as the coach of the Hurricanes. In 1989, the Dallas Cowboys finished with a 1–15 record, and selected Troy Aikman with the number one pick in the draft. Scouts compared Troy to John Elway and Dan Marino for his physical ability. But what Coach Johnson liked most about Troy was his work ethic and leadership skills.

**Aikman scrambles out of the pocket
like the best of them!**

With Troy leading the way, the Cowboys improved to a remarkable 7–9 record in 1990, and missed the play-offs by only one game. Troy threw for an NFL one-game rookie-record of 379 yards against the Phoenix Cardinals, and became the first Cowboy since 1987 to throw four touch-downs in a game. This was a feat he accomplished against the Los Angeles Rams on December 3.

His next season proved to be even better. Growing more comfortable with the Cowboys' offense, Troy led his team to an 11–5 record and a wild card spot in the play-offs. Although the Cowboys lost to the Detroit Lions, after beating the Chicago Bears 17–13, it was clear that they were well on their way to the championship that owner Jerry Jones had promised. Troy ended the season by completing a club record of 65.3 percent of his passes and by earning his first trip to the Pro-Bowl.

The Cowboys were the "team to watch" at the start of the 1992 season. They began the season winning eight of their first nine games, and finished with a 13–3 record. Troy completed 63.8 percent of his passes while throwing for an amazing 3,445 yards, with just 14 interceptions.

As the play-offs began, Troy, as usual, was ready for the challenge. Displaying his characteristic coolness, Troy led the Cowboys to a 34–10 victory over the Philadelphia Eagles in the divisional play-offs, followed by a 30–20 win over the San Francisco 49ers in the NFC Championship game.

This set the stage for Troy's biggest test yet as a professional. In the Super Bowl, Troy was facing the Buffalo Bills' Jim Kelly, regarded as the NFL's premier quarterback. Most experts thought that Troy was in over his head. But Troy proved them wrong. After falling behind early in the first quarter, Troy led a fierce Dallas charge with a splendid combination of short passing and pinpoint bombs that crushed the Bills 52–17. With this triumph, Troy Aikman established himself as the best young quarterback in the game today.

CHAPTER FOUR

Jennifer Capriati

◇ ◇ ◇ ◇ ◇ ◇ ◇ ◇

Teen Tennis Star

Jennifer Capriati burst onto the professional tennis scene when she was 13. Although no one her age had ever been a pro before, Jennifer made it all the way to the finals of her first event before being stopped.

Since then, Jennifer has continued to amaze the tennis world. She won her first professional tournament when she was 14, and played in the semifinals of the U.S. Open and Wimbledon when she was 15. In 1992, she won a gold medal in the Olympic games in Barcelona, Spain. And, she's done all of this while trying to be a normal teenager—even if most teenagers don't earn millions of dollars a year.

Tall, dark, and striking, Jennifer is a true prodigy. She inherited her tennis talent, as well as her determination, from her dad, Stefano Capriati. In his native Italy, he was a soccer star who turned to tennis when an injury cut short his kicking career. Stefano loved tennis and, when he married, taught

Jennifer Capriati returns the ball cross court.

his wife, Denise, to play as well. The two were on the courts all the time. It was only natural that when their firstborn arrived, she'd toddle over to the baseline as well.

"My parents were always on the tennis courts and had no place to leave me, so they brought me with them. I just kind of picked up a racquet and hit tennis balls all over the place. My dad noticed I had good coordination, so he started giving me lessons."

When Jennifer was four, the family moved from Italy to America and put down roots in Florida, not far from where superstar Chris Evert's father worked as a tennis coach. Stefano asked Jimmy Evert to coach Jennifer and the older pro accepted. Soon Jennifer proved what her parents already suspected—she was a quick learner and a determined player.

As she grew, Jennifer began a rigorous training program. She'd attend private school in the morning, come home by noon for several hours of practice, and then go back to school in the evening.

In addition to on-court practice and homework, Jennifer did rigorous exercises every day. These included throwing nerf footballs to coordinate her shoulder muscles and working out with a hula hoop to improve hip strength. Push-ups (35 per minute) and sit-ups (60 per minute) were also part of the routine.

Naturally, Jennifer joined the junior tennis circuit as soon as she was eligible, and by age 12, a year before she turned pro, she won the U.S. Tennis Association's Girls' 18 and Under Hard Court and Clay Championships. She also went on to win the U.S. and French Jr. Opens.

In her first year playing professionally, when no one expected much of her, Jennifer took each match as it came.

**Olympic gold medal winner Jennifer Capriati
in a victorious cheer.**

If she won, great. If she didn't, well, there would be other matches.

All that changed in 1991, when Jennifer beat one of tennis' all-time great players, Martina Navratilova, in the quarterfinals at Wimbledon.

"I don't know if that win changed me as a person," Jennifer says. "But inside it made me realize I could be a top player."

While she was trying to grow as a tennis player, Jennifer was also growing in other ways. She traded her old Bart Simpson tee shirts for black jackets and boots, added more holes to her already-pierced ears, and started spending more time by herself. She listened to Guns N' Roses or Metallica and began checking out all the cute ball boys.

On the courts, tennis suddenly seemed to be getting too serious for Jennifer. In her third year as a pro, Jennifer lost a heartbreaking match to Gabriella Sabatini at the Australian Open, where she had hoped to win her first Grand Slam title.

At the same time, Jennifer was finding the courses at her private high school growing tougher, and her usual straight A's began to suffer.

Jennifer admits that trying to be a tennis star while growing up is a lot for a teenager to handle.

"I think everyone goes through it but I'm dealing with tennis too," explains Jennifer. "Plus, you've got the added pressure of trying to be accepted by your friends, dealing with math and chemistry teachers, and dealing with rules at home. I mean, it's a lot."

But winning the 1992 Olympic gold medal was a turning point for Jennifer for two reasons. First of all, she won the gold for her own country, proudly wearing the U.S.

uniform. "I kept thinking it would be so cool to be up there on the medal stand, like, really unbelievable," recalls Jennifer. "And here I got the chance."

And secondly, Jennifer won her medal by beating rival Steffi Graf for the first time in her career.

After that win, Jennifer started playing matches wearing a white hat emblazoned with the American flag. But despite the victory over Steffi at Barcelona, Jennifer still has trouble beating her at championship matches.

Jennifer lost to Steffi in the semifinals at the 1992 Virginia Slims Championships and in the quarterfinals of the 1993 Australian Open. Still, Jennifer, whose career slump seems to be over, believes her turn to be number one will come.

"I'm a lot happier now," she says. "I'm very happy with my game and I'm confident about the future."

Steffi Graf, look out!

CHAPTER FIVE

Mario Lemieux

❖ ❖ ❖ ❖ ❖ ❖ ❖ ❖

Superstar on Ice

Mario Lemieux was born in Quebec, Canada, in 1965, and by the time he was three years old, he was skating faster than most six year olds. At age nine, Mario was the best hockey player in the teen division, and when he was 15, he quit school to play hockey full time for the Laval Voisins of the Quebec Major Junior Hockey League.

Earning a mere $35 per week, Mario soon achieved "legend status," as he shattered every junior hockey record in Canada. He scored an incredible 282 points when he was 17, netting 133 goals to go along with 149 assists.

At 6'4" and 200 pounds, no one would dare get in Lemieux's way. As one NHL scout put it, "If Mario couldn't go around you, he'd go right through you." His size and speed, coupled with an uncanny ability to find the open man, made Mario virtually unstoppable on ice.

The Pittsburgh Penguins finished the 1983–84 season with the worst record in the NHL and, getting the first

Mario Lemieux slices across the ice.

pick in the 1984 amateur draft, took Mario. The Penguins were a franchise on the brink of folding, and Lemieux was their last hope for survival. Experts were so sure that Mario was destined to become a superstar, that the Minnesota North Stars offered Pittsburgh any 12 players on their team for him.

Mario's career with the Penguins got off to a shaky start when he threatened to sit out his first season if Pittsburgh didn't give him the contract he wanted. This did not make Mario very popular with the fans. With their backs up against the wall, Pittsburgh management gave in to his demands, and made Mario the highest paid rookie ever, signing him to a $600,000 contract.

Mario scored the first goal of his NHL career with his very first shot against the Boston Bruins. All money matters were soon forgotten, and Penguin fans fell in love with Mario. By the end of the 1984–85 season, attendance in the "Igloo" had doubled. As one general manager put it, "Mario saved hockey in Pittsburgh."

But while Mario was welcomed with open arms in Pittsburgh, life in the NHL was quite a change from the junior hockey league he was used to. Although, at age 20, Mario had grown to 6'5" and weighed nearly 225 pounds, for the first time in his career he suffered injuries, had bad games, and was criticized by the press. This hurt Mario a great deal, but instead of letting it get him down, it only made him more determined to prove his critics wrong. He finished the year with 43 goals and 57 assists, making him the third rookie in NHL history to score 100 points. He easily won the Calder Trophy as the NHL's Rookie of the Year, and was a unanimous choice for the All-Rookie team.

Mario Lemieux brings the Stanley Cup home for the Penguins.

In his second season, Mario began to blossom into the player the Penguins hoped he would be. He finished the season with 141 points, and comparisons were starting to be made between him and the Edmonton Oilers' Wayne Gretzky.

In 1987, Lemieux and Gretzky played together for the first time in the Canada Cup, something Lemieux had always dreamed of doing. Playing alongside his childhood idol, Mario elevated his game to even greater heights. He scored 11 goals in the series, as Canada beat the Soviet Union 6–5 in the finals.

Growing more confident with each passing year, Mario became the third player in NHL history to score over 150 points when he totaled 168 during the 1987–88 season. This earned him his first Hart Trophy as the league's Most Valuable Player. More important than that, the Penguins finished with a 36–35–9 record. It was the first time in nearly a decade that they finished with a winning record, though they still fell short of making the play-offs.

Despite all of his scoring records, Mario had not brought a Stanley Cup to Pittsburgh, and the fans were once again growing restless. And then in the 1990–91 season, Mario began having back problems. Things got so bad that he only played in 26 games. But remarkably, the Penguins made the play-offs without him. And then, with the added rest of not playing during the season, Lemieux led the Penguins to their first Stanley Cup victory over the Minnesota North Stars. For his effort, Mario was named MVP of the championship series.

The 1991–92 season started off tragically for the Penguins, as their coach Bob Johnson died of brain cancer. But Mario and the team rallied. Although Lemieux played in only 64 games because of reoccurring back problems, he won his third scoring title, tallying 131 points. And the Penguins won their second consecutive Stanley Cup, sweeping the Chicago Blackhawks 4–0.

Unfortunately, Mario's greatest challenge lay ahead of him, as the 1993 season got underway. He was diagnosed with Hodgkins Disease (a form of cancer) during a routine physical examination. Many experts thought that his career was over. Showing more courage than anyone could ever have imagined, not only did Mario return to the Penguin lineup after missing only 23 games, but he won his fourth scoring title, edging out the Buffalo Sabres' Pat LaFontaine.

Although the Penguins lost to the Islanders in the play-offs, ending their bid for a third straight Stanley Cup, Mario showed the world that he was a champion on and off the ice.

CHAPTER SIX

Teresa Edwards

❖ ❖ ❖ ❖ ❖ ❖ ❖ ❖

The First Lady of Basketball

Teresa Edwards is most often referred to as "the Michael Jordan" of women's basketball. She is a slick ball handler, a prolific scorer, and plays defense much the same way that Jordan does—in your face. But when she was growing up in Cairo, Georgia, Teresa's mother never thought that she would be good enough to play organized basketball.

Teresa would spend most of every afternoon shooting baskets through an old bicycle rim that was nailed to a pine tree on her block. And even though Teresa was better than most of the boys she played against, her mother thought that she was too slow and too short to be any good at basketball. That all changed when Teresa made Washington Middle School's seventh-grade team. She quickly became the best player on the team, and at the end of ninth grade, Teresa won an invitation to the National Sports Festival in Colorado.

**Theresa Edwards dribbles past Canada's
Misty Thomas and scores!**

By her senior year, Teresa was 5'11" and weighed 145 pounds. She was one of the most sought-after female basketball players in the country, but there was never a doubt in her mind as to which college she wanted to attend. It was the University of Georgia.

As the 1983 season began, it didn't take long for Teresa to establish herself as the best basketball player on the team. Shooting just under 50 percent from the field, Teresa averaged 13.0 points per game, dished out 100 assists, and showed her durability by playing in all of the Bull Dogs' 33 games. Because of her strong showing, Teresa earned her second invitation to the National Sports Festival, where she won the Most Valuable Player award. Later that year, Teresa was selected as a member of the Junior Pan-American team, which won the gold medal in the Pan-Am games.

As a sophomore, Teresa's numbers improved dramatically, due to her hard work and uncanny ability to make everyone she played with a better basketball player. Teresa shot 55 percent from the field, had 81 steals, shot 80 percent from the foul line, and handed out 189 assists, while averaging 14.1 points per game. These numbers earned Teresa her first All-South Eastern Conference team selection. But, more importantly, she was also invited to try out for the United States Olympic team.

With such stars as Pam McGee, Cheryl Miller, and Lynette Woodard trying out, Teresa never thought she had a chance to make the team. But when the final cut was made, Teresa, at age 19, was the youngest, and perhaps the happiest, member of the 1984 Olympic team. Though she saw little action, averaging only 2.5 points per game and 2.0 rebounds, Teresa came home with her first gold medal, as the United States defeated South Korea, 85–55. The

Theresa Edwards goes to the basket for the USA.

international experience proved to be invaluable to her when she returned to Georgia for her junior year. That season she averaged 15.5 points per game, 2.8 rebounds, and was named a consensus All-American for the first time in her career.

In 1986, as a senior at Georgia, Teresa averaged nearly 20 points per game, shot 80 percent from the foul line, and was named a consensus All-American for the second straight year. She finished her career at Georgia as the all-time leader in assists (653) and steals (342), and was third in scoring with 1,989 points. At the end of the season, she was selected to both the United States World Championship team and the United States Goodwill team. Earning a gold medal with both teams, Teresa was starting to gain international recognition as one of the best female basketball players in the world.

Although women's basketball is very popular at the collegiate level, many attempts to have a professional women's league have failed in the United States. Playing basketball is all that Teresa Edwards ever wanted to do, so with nowhere else to play, she left the United States to play professionally in Italy and Japan.

In 1988, Teresa took time out from her professional obligations to play for the gold-medal winning United States Olympic Team. Where in 1984 she hardly saw any playing time, in 1988, Teresa was the most valuable player on the United States team. She averaged 16.6 points per game, while leading the team in field goal percentage, assists, and steals. And while 1992 proved to be a disappointment, as the United States had to settle for a bronze medal, Teresa Edwards says that she is looking forward to playing for the United States again in 1996, and promises to bring home the gold!

Ken Griffey at bat. It's a double!

CHAPTER SEVEN

Ken Griffey, Jr.

✧ ✧ ✧ ✧ ✧ ✧ ✧ ✧

Baseball's All-Around Best

Ken Griffey, Jr., grew up in Cincinnati, Ohio, where his father, Ken Griffey, Sr., was an All-Star outfielder for the Cincinnati Reds. Ken Jr. would often go to Reds' games and sit on the bench next to his father and other superstars, such as Pete Rose, Johnny Bench, and Joe Morgan. It was here that Ken Jr. found out what it took to be a major league baseball player, and he put it all to good use.

Ken attended Moller High School, where he was an All-State football and baseball player. In 1986 and 1987, he was voted the top high school baseball player in the country. Ken loved playing football as much as baseball, and it was a tough decision for him when the Seattle Mariners made him the number one pick in the country in the 1987 amateur baseball draft. At the same time, Ken also received hundreds of scholarships to play college football. But in the end, he chose baseball, and the Mariners are sure glad that he did!

Ken Griffey, Jr. hits another one out of the park!

From the moment Ken put on a Mariners uniform, his coaches agreed that he was destined to become a superstar. There was nothing Ken couldn't do. He could run, hit for power and average, and catch any ball that came his way. In his first full year of professional baseball, Ken hit .313, drove in 40 runs, hit 14 home runs, and stole 13 bases for the Mariners' Single A ball club. And he did it all at the age of 17!

It was clear that Ken belonged in the major leagues, but the Mariners didn't want to rush him. So Ken started the next season playing Double A ball, where he hit .338, knocked in 42 runs, and banged out 74 hits in just 58 games. Ken finished the year with the Mariners' Triple A club, where he hit a respectable .279 in 17 games.

At the start of the 1989 exhibition season, Ken was invited to attend the Mariners' major league camp. By the time the exhibition season was over, and the final rosters were decided, Ken not only made the team but was penciled in as the starting center fielder on opening day!

Ken was an immediate hit with his teammates, as well as with the fans. His strong work ethic, which he learned from his father and the rest of the Cincinnati Reds, earned him the respect of the veterans on the Mariners, while the other rookies looked up to him for leadership and guidance.

Since their expansion year, the Mariners always had trouble selling tickets. That all changed with Ken in the lineup. He was, as one sportscaster put it, "pure excitement."

In his first time at bat in the major league, Ken gave the Mariners crowd a taste of things to come when he doubled off of Oakland A's pitching ace Dave Stewart. A few games later, at just 19 years old, Ken hit his first major league home run, a towering drive off of Eric King of the Chicago White Sox.

Ken was on a record-breaking course in his rookie year when he broke a bone in his hand while diving for a line drive in the outfield. Even though he missed 35 games, Ken still finished the season hitting .264, while banging out 16 home runs and driving in 61 runs.

During the off-season, the Mariners acquired Ken Griffey, Sr., and on August 31, 1990, the two Griffeys became the first father and son to play together in the same game. And then, on September 14, they hit back-to-back home runs against the California Angels.

It proved to be a record-breaking year for Ken Jr. He became the first Mariner ever elected to the starting lineup of an All-Star game, earned his first Gold Glove award for his defensive ability, and hit .300, while driving in a club-leading 80 runs.

Before the 1991 season began, Ken Jr. embarked on a weight training program, and by the time the season started, he had gained 20 pounds of muscle and was even faster on the base paths than the year before! Ken's hard work paid off, as he was the top vote-getter for the All-Star game, edging out such superstars as Jose Canseco, Kirby Pucket, and Dave Winfield. Ken knocked in his 100th run on September 30, and at age 22, became the youngest player to do so since Al Kaline in 1956. Ken finished the year breaking several Mariner's records. He hit .327, smacked out 42 doubles, and had a slugging percentage of over .500. He received his second straight Gold Glove award and was selected to the AP's post season All-Star team.

Ken's numbers continued to rise in 1992, as he hit 27 home runs, scored 83 times, and drove in 103 runs. The Mariners rewarded him with a multi-year contract, making him the game's youngest millionaire, and making sure that he stays in a Mariners uniform for years to come.

Manon is as beautiful as she is athletic.

CHAPTER EIGHT

Manon Rheaume

❖ ❖ ❖ ❖ ❖ ❖ ❖ ❖

Hockey's Princess

She has been stopping boys' pucks since she was five years old. So when Manon Rheaume took to the ice during an exhibition game with the Tampa Bay Lightning squad in September 1992, she did what came naturally. She stopped pucks—only this time they were being fired by professional male hockey players.

That night, as fans shouted her name, Manon became the first woman to ever play in one of the four major professional sports leagues. The French Canadian goalie played well enough to win a three-year contract with the expansion team's minor league affiliate and a shot at being the first woman to join the National Hockey League.

"I don't do this for the publicity," says Manon, 20, who spoke mainly French until last year. "I just like hockey. I want to get better. I want to learn."

Manon began learning when she was three. She started to skate outside her house on a little rink her father created each year using a water pipe from the house. Manon's older brothers, Martin and Pascal, took shots and she tried to stop them.

When she was five, Manon and her mother went to watch her brothers play in a local tournament at their home in Lac-Beauport, Quebec. But the team's goalie didn't show up, and her father, the coach, needed someone to tend the net.

Manon asked to play. Her father laughed—but he also strapped pads on her and sent her out onto the ice.

"He said 'Why not? You take shots from your brothers at home,'" recalls Manon.

Right from the beginning, Manon loved the sport. She played with boys' teams and often outplayed the boys.

"Every year, the boys found it special to have a girl on the team, but after the first day, they didn't look at me as a girl," Manon says. "They looked at me as a player."

When she wasn't skating, Manon took ballet, played baseball, and skied. But by age 12, Manon was playing hockey year-round.

"I didn't just *play* hockey," she says. "It was my passion." Manon played in Canada's youth leagues and kept right on stopping pucks. She dove at them, blocked them, and snatched them out of the air with her glove.

But, when she turned 15, she ran into her first barrier. No teenaged girl had ever played for Canada's best junior league, the step before professional hockey. It looked as if Manon's days of playing with the boys were over.

Manon then turned to women's teams. In April 1992, she led the Canadian National Women's Team to its gold-medal finish in Finland. But before that championship, she got one more opportunity to play with the boys. The Trois-

Rivieres' starting goaltender became injured and the team needed another backup goalie. Manon, whose boyfriend belonged to the team, was asked to play. Although Manon sat on the bench for the first two games, she took over the goal in the third game and became the first woman ever to play in Canada's Junior A League.

In that game, she faced male hockey players who set out to test whether she'd scare easily. Players jammed the goal and some shot pucks up high toward her head. But Manon didn't mind those tactics. To her, they meant that the male players were treating her like any other goalie. And that's how Manon wants to be treated.

"I have to deal with this," she says. "They do this with other goaltenders. If I have a chance to play, I'm going to play." One of the pucks shot at Manon during the junior game hit her face mask, giving her a gash that would later take four stitches to close. But Manon kept playing until she was taken out.

"I continued to play," she says, "because I didn't want anyone to say I stopped because I was a girl."

News of Manon's play reached ex-Ranger Phil Esposito, the G. M. and president of the Tampa Bay team. He invited her to try out for the Lightning, partly because he had heard she was good, and partly because he knew her tryout would attract attention for his new team.

Manon wasted no time proving to the male players that they had better take her seriously. During the first day of tryouts, Manon was the only goalie to stop all the pucks shot at her.

"She stoned us," recalls player Brent Gretzky, hockey superstar Wayne Gretzky's younger brother.

Manon's chance to break another barrier came during

Manon Rheaume is hockey's first female professional goalie.

the first period of an exhibition game against the St. Louis Blues. She faced nine shots and gave up only two goals.

Esposito says Manon earned the contract to Atlanta. "She did well during the preseason, and she earned a spot on the roster," he says.

Although she is very good, Manon knows she's not yet ready to play daily in the NHL. "What is more realistic is to learn," she explains. "I never thought before of playing in the NHL. That's just too far ahead. It's not important to be the first woman, second, third. I just say I'm going to try. When you love the sport, you want to play."

Until recently, Manon hasn't had the opportunity most of her fellow players have had to train regularly. She thinks that may have hurt her. But as a player for the minor league Atlanta Knights, Manon is now getting the chance to practice daily instead of twice a week.

Although speed and reflexes are more important to a goalie than strength, Manon, at 5'6" and 135 pounds, knows she has to build up her muscles and endurance. Her daily schedule is tough: practice, followed by extra drills, followed by more exercise. Besides aerobics, she lifts weights and does six different kinds of sit-ups. Manon no longer has much time to play softball or tennis, or to go shopping.

Playing in the minor leagues is tougher than anything Manon has done before: The players are rougher, and the shots are harder. But, the defensemen guarding the goal are also better. That helps. And after all the years of playing with her brothers and other guys, Manon is comfortable with her fellow teammates.

"They come over to encourage me," she says. "If I do something wrong, the two other goaltenders say, 'Do it like this.' I learn with the guys."

Rheaume says the way she's played in practice and intrasquad games shows she's not being kept on for publicity. "I can skate," she says. "I can stop a puck. I haven't been an embarrassment."

In December 1992, Manon became the first woman to play in a regular season professional hockey match. She guarded the net for the Knights against a minor league team out of Salt Lake City, Utah. During her second period play, she stopped three shots and allowed one goal.

"I was a little bit nervous," Manon recalls. "You learn by your mistakes. I'll learn what to do."

Manon is thrilled that many hockey fans are supporting her. During the December game, the crowd gave her a standing ovation when she skated onto the ice to take the net.

No matter how much action Manon sees with the Knights, practicing with a pro team is making her a better goalie. And that will give her an edge if, as expected, women's ice hockey is added to the Olympics in 1998 or 2002.

"If they have women's ice hockey in the 1998 Olympics," she notes, "I'll be ready. It's very important."

Meanwhile, for Manon it's enough to be playing the sport she loves every day.

CHAPTER NINE

The Official Sports Heroes and Heroines Trivia Quiz

❖ ❖ ❖ ❖ ❖ ❖ ❖ ❖ ❖

Multiple Choice

1. Which college did Shaquille O'Neal attend?
   a. U.C.L.A.
   b. L.S.U.
   c. U.A.B.
   d. U.S.C.

2. Which player does Mario Lemieux wear his number in tribute to?
   a. Mark Messier
   b. Gordie Howe
   c. Wayne Gretzky
   d. Mike Bossy

Shaq and Patrick Ewing of the Knicks go one on one.

3. Which year was Troy Aikman picked first in the NFL draft?
   a. 1989
   b. 1988
   c. 1991
   d. 1987

4. Who is the coach of the Dallas Cowboys?
   a. Bill Parcells
   b. Dan Reeves
   c. Chuck Knox
   d. Jimmy Johnson

5. In which race did Gail Devers win a gold medal in the 1992 Olympics?
   a. 100-meter dash
   b. 200-meter dash
   c. 100-meter hurdles
   d. 400-meter relay

6. Who won the 1992 Olympic gold medal in women's tennis?
   a. Steffi Graf
   b. Jennifer Capriati
   c. Martina Navratilova
   d. Monica Seles

7. In which year did Teresa Edwards first participate in the Olympics?
   a. 1988
   b. 1990
   c. 1984
   d. 1980

8. Who were the first father-and-son baseball players to play in the Major Leagues in the same game?
   a. Dale and Yogi Berra
   b. Barry and Bobby Bonds
   c. Ken Griffey, Sr. and Jr.
   d. Kirt and Kendal Smith

9. Which team does Shaquille O'Neal play for?
   a. The Miami Heat
   b. The Charlotte Hornets
   c. The Orlando Magic
   d. The Minnesota Timberwolves

10. How many points did Mario Lemieux score in his rookie season in the NHL?
    a. 96
    b. 100
    c. 101
    d. 119

11. Which disease almost ruined Gail Devers' track career?
    a. Graves' disease
    b. bronchial asthma
    c. whooping cough
    d. heartburn

12. What was the Dallas Cowboys record in 1992?
    a. 11–5
    b. 9–7
    c. 12–4
    d. 13–3

True or False

1. After his sophomore year in college, Troy Aikman transferred from Nebraska to U.C.L.A. ___T___F

2. Gail Devers won a gold medal in the 1992 Olympics in the 100-meter hurdles. ___T___F

3. Shaquille O'Neal started at center for the Eastern Squad in the 1992 All-Star game. ___T___F

4. Manon Rheaume plays forward for the Tampa Bay Lightning. ___T___F

5. As a junior hockey player, Mario Lemieux scored 282 points in one season, the most ever in league history. ___T___F

6. Teresa Edwards was the first American basketball player, male or female, to participate in three Olympiads. ___T___F

7. Ken Griffey, Jr., was the first player selected in the 1987 baseball draft by the Seattle Mariners. ___T___F

8. Gail Devers won a silver medal in the 100-meter dash in the 1988 Olympics. ___T___F

9. Troy Aikman led the U.C.L.A. Bruins to an Aloha Bowl victory. ___T___F

10. Jennifer Capriati has never been ranked #1 in the world. ___T___F

11. Shaquille O'Neal's name means "big warrior." ___T___F

12. Teresa Edwards played for the University of Oklahoma from 1983–1986. ___T___F

Matching

Do you know all there is to know about your favorite sports heroes and heroines? If so, then you'll have no problem completing the matching puzzle below. Just put the letter of the match next to the number.

_____ 1. Goalie

_____ 2. Ken Griffey, Sr.

_____ 3. 1984, 1988, 1992
Olympics

_____ 4. 66

_____ 5. Troy Aikman

_____ 6. Shaquille O'Neal

_____ 7. Graves' disease

_____ 8. Moller High School

_____ 9. 99

_____10. 1992 Super Bowl
Champions

_____11. 1992 Olympic Gold

_____12. Pittsburgh Penguins
Medal Tennis

A. Dallas Cowboys

B. Jennifer Capriati

C. U.C.L.A.

D. Gail Devers

E. Mario Lemieux

F. Cincinnati Reds

G. Manon Rheaume

H. Ken Griffey, Jr.

I. Teresa Edwards

J. The "Igloo"

K. Wayne Gretzky

L. Shaq

ANSWERS:

Multiple Choice
1. b; 2. c; 3. a; 4. d; 5. a; 6. b; 7. c; 8. c; 9. c; 10. b;
11. a; 12. d.

True or False
1. F; 2. F; 3. T; 4. F; 5. T; 6. T; 7. T; 8. F; 9. T;
10. T; 11. F; 12. F.

Matching
1. G; 2. F; 3. I; 4. E; 5. C; 6. L; 7. D; 8. H; 9. K;
10. A; 11. B; 12. J.